I CAN DO THAT!
Creative play for can-do kids
STICK

T0053448

How to Use This Book

Most of the activities in this book are easy enough for your child to complete without help, but you should provide instructions.

Play Again and Again!

The stickers are reusable, so your child can do the activities again and again.

Build Skills While Playing

Playing with stickers is a marvelous way to hone fine motor skills, hand-eye coordination, and spatial relations. Your child will use stickers to solve mazes, play matching and counting games, and decorate pictures. At the same time, he or she will:

- practice skills like decision making and thinking ahead
- enhance the ability to sort and match objects by size, shape, and color
- develop observational skills
- strengthen counting skills
- build confidence
- increase vocabulary
- exercise creativity

Play Together!

Studies show that children learn best when they are engaged with an adult. After your child finishes an activity, talk about the images on the page. Ask your child to point to and name the animals, objects, colors, or shapes on the page. Ask which items are the biggest or smallest or which food looks the tastiest.

GARDEN VISITORS

Put a butterfly near each big flower. Add 3 little flowers wherever you like.

SWEET TREATS

Add scoops of ice cream until each cone has the same number of scoops.

COUNT WITH APPLES, 1, 2, 3

Look at the numbers below. Count the number of red dots in each row.
Then, put the same number of apple stickers on each row.

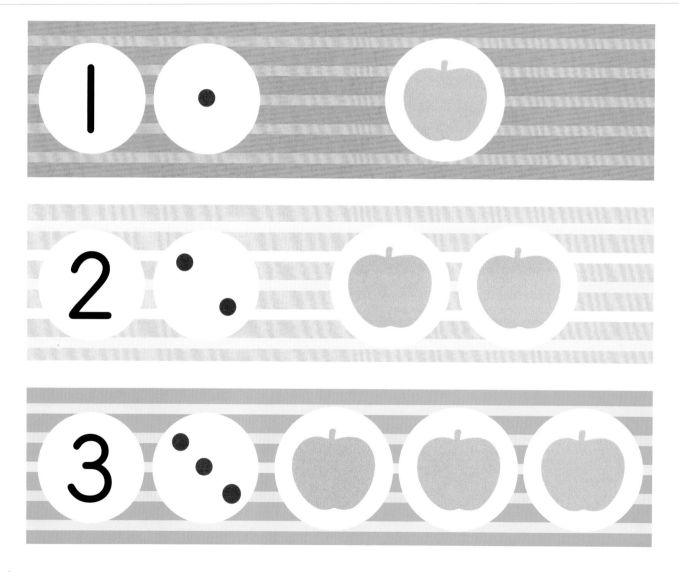

DESSERT MAZE

Help Bear go from ➡ to ➡. Find a path where Bear can pick up each treat on his way without backtracking. Place the matching stickers on each circle as you go.

SPRING SHOWERS

Uh-oh! It is raining! Help each child stay dry by putting an open umbrella over each closed umbrella. Make sure the umbrellas match. Then, add more raindrops to the sky and more little animals to the scene.

PLAYTIME AT THE PLAYGROUND

Place a sticker in each box to fill in the playground pictures below.

GET READY FOR ART CLASS

Put the stickers on the desks so each child has 2 sheets of paper,
2 crayons, and I pair of scissors.

2 sheets of colored paper

2 crayons

I pair of scissors

COUNTING BEARS AND LOLLIPOPS

Use the stickers to fill in the boxes. Make sure the number of bears and the number of lollipops in each row matches the number at the beginning of each row.

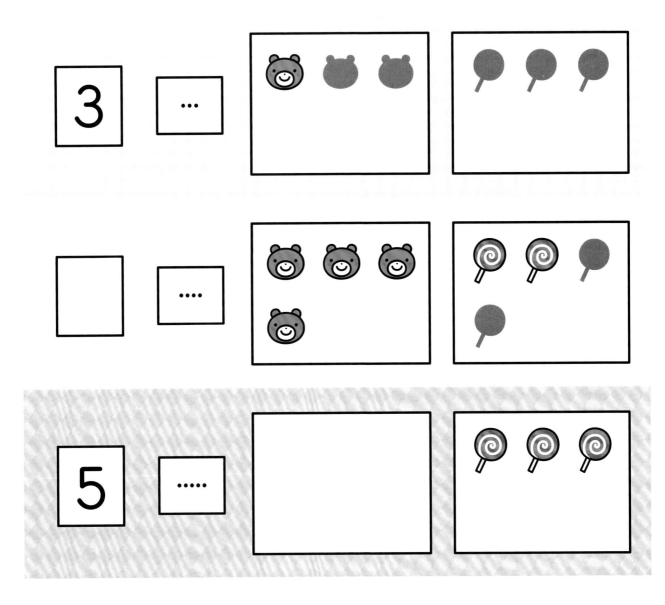

PANCAKE PARTY!

Give pancakes and a fork to each animal. Make sure the pancake sizes match.

LET'S COUNT TO 9!

Count the number of items in each box below. Put the matching number sticker in the ■.

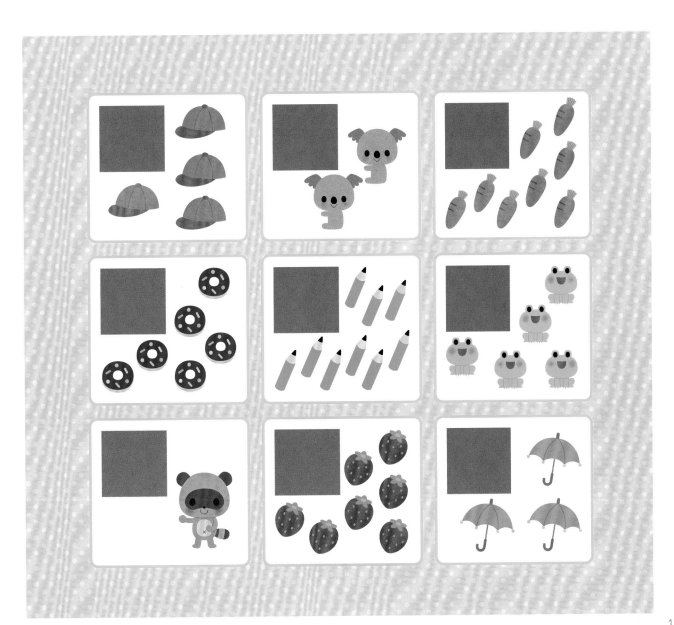

A TRIP TO THE AMUSEMENT PARK

Go through the amusement park from ➡️ to ➡️. Put the ride stickers on the matching shadows as you go. Which ride do you want to go on?

JUNGLE WALK

Go through the jungle from ➡ to ➡ . What animals do you see?
Put the stickers on the matching shadows as you go.

MATCH THE ANIMALS

What kinds of creatures will you see at the pond? Put each sticker on its matching shadow.

BIG CHICKS, LITTLE CHICKS

Put a chick sticker in each eggshell. Put the small chicks in the small eggshells and the big chicks in the big eggshells. Can you cluck like a chick?

LET'S MAKE A CHEESEBURGER

Go through the maze from ➡ to ➡. As you go, place the matching sticker on each item you need to make a cheeseburger (lettuce, hamburger patty, tomato, cheese, bun).

MAKE MATCHING PLATES

Add cookie and candy stickers to each plate until each plate matches the example. How many cookies are on each plate? How many candies?

EXAMPLE

GONE FISHING

Follow the fishing lines to find the fish each animal has caught.
Put the matching sticker in the fish tank next to each animal.

CAKE PARTY!

Decorate the cakes with strawberries, chocolates, and candy.
Then, put a fork next to the desserts that look the tastiest.

SHIPS AHOY!

Use the stickers to fill in the maze. Each sticker goes on the ▢ with the matching ★. Then, draw a line from ➡ to ➡ to solve the maze.

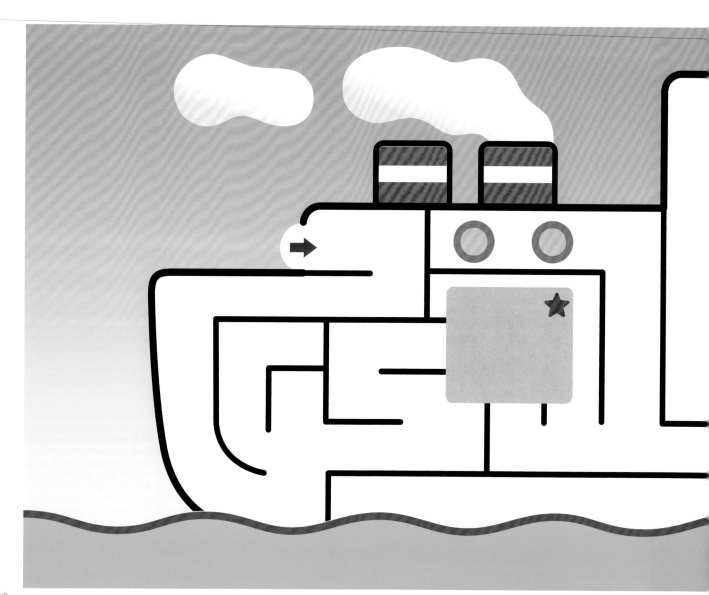

WHAT A BUSY DAY!

What is happening in each scene? Find a sticker that shows items that can be used for each activity, and place it on the matching ■.

WHO IS RIDING THE RIDES?

Place the stickers on the matching shapes to complete this fun scene.

COUNT THE FROGS

Put frog stickers on the  below. Then, put the number stickers on the ▭ so the number of frogs on each lily pad matches the number beneath it.

MATCH THE VEHICLE PARTS

Each circle below shows part of a vehicle. Place the matching sticker on the ▢.
Say the names of each vehicle as you go (ambulance, police car, fire truck, excavator).

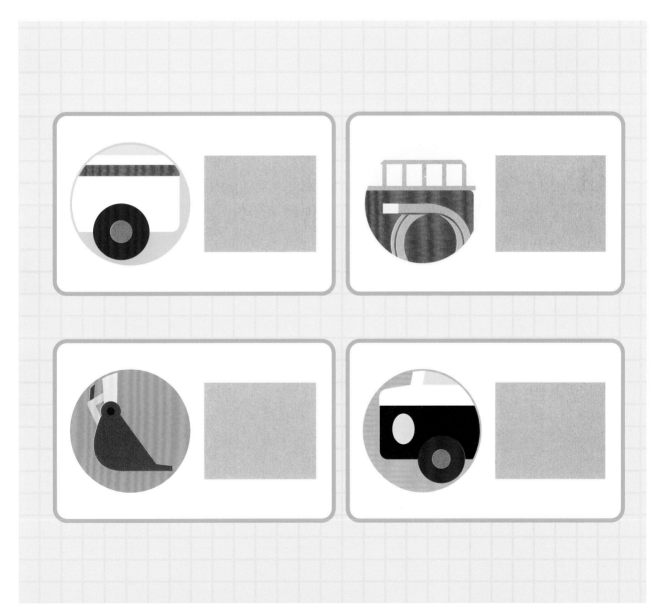

A SNACK FOR EACH ANIMAL

The chipmunks want to eat acorns. Put an acorn for each chipmunk on the plate. If there are any acorn stickers left over, place them in the basket. Do the same for the monkeys and apples and the rabbits and carrots.

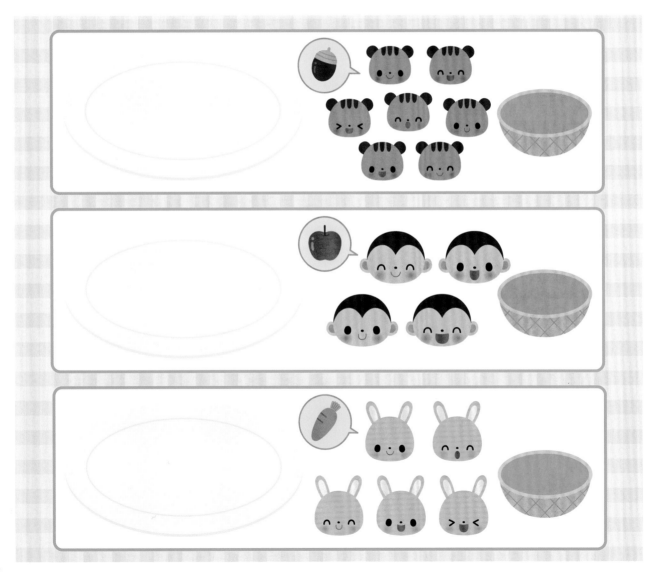

PLENTY OF FISH IN THE SEA

Add fish stickers to the page until there are 5 big fish and 8 small fish.

MOLE'S UNDERGROUND MAZE

Help get the guests to Mole's graduation party. Put each sticker on the ▢ with the matching ★. Then, draw a line from ➡ to ➡ to solve the maze.

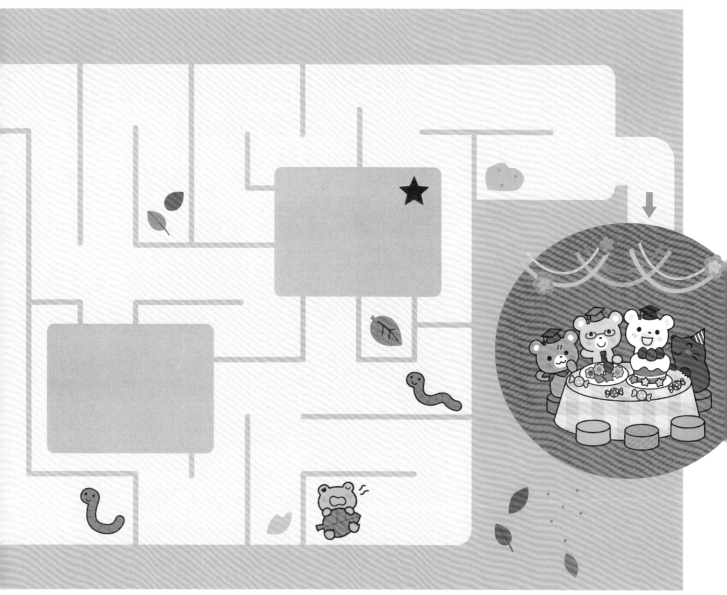

ROBOT TWINS!

Put the stickers on the page to create two robots that look exactly alike.

COMPLETE THE PICTURES

Put the matching sticker on the page to fill in each picture. If you can't tell which scene a sticker belongs to, look at its shape.

ARE THERE MORE GIRAFFES OR ZEBRAS?

Place a zebra sticker in a blue box for each zebra you see in the picture. Place a giraffe sticker in a pink box for each giraffe you see. Put a sticker in the ☐ below to show which animal there are more of. Then, write the number in the ⬭.

There are more: ☐

How many?

ARE THERE FEWER DRAGONFLIES OR BUTTERFLIES?

Place a dragonfly sticker in a pink box for each dragonfly you see in the picture. Place a butterfly sticker in a blue box for each butterfly you see. Put a sticker in the ☐ below to show which animal there are fewer of. Then, write the number in the ⬭.

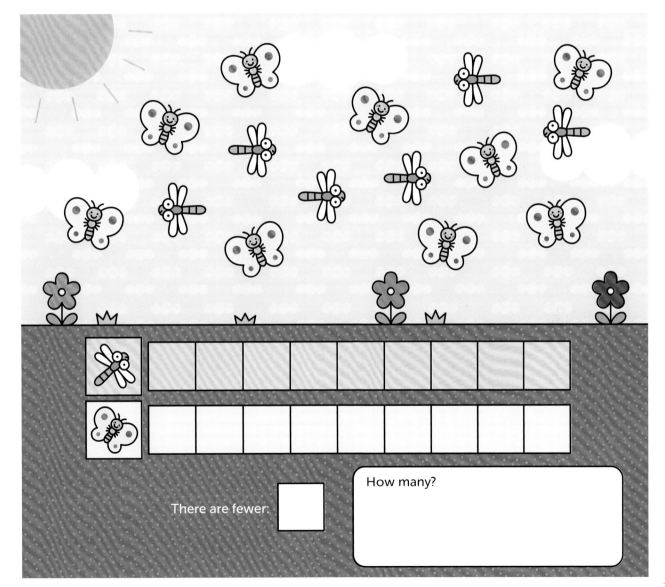

There are fewer: ☐

How many?

WHICH WAY SHOULD BEAR GO?

Bear needs help to get to Bunny's house. Put each sticker on the ▢ with the matching ★. Then, draw a line from ➡ to ➡ to solve the maze.

WHOSE HAT IS THAT?

Look at each person below. Find a hat sticker that matches each person's clothing and put it on that person's head.

RAINY DAY ROMP

Add stickers to the picture to keep the girl from getting wet.

HELP MONKEY GO HOME

Draw a line from ➡ to ➡ . Always go in the direction of the larger number. Each time you choose a path, put a sticker on the page with the matching number of fruits.

HAPPY BIRTHDAY!

Decorate each cake so the number of candles matches the age of each child.

FOLLOW THE ACORNS

Complete the maze by drawing a line from acorn to acorn.
Put a squirrel sticker on each acorn as you go.

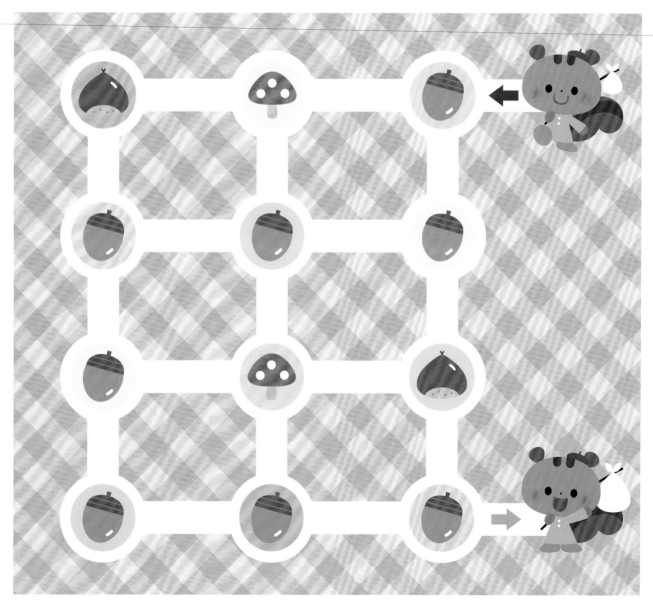

FLY BY THE FLOWER BOX

Put a butterfly sticker next to each flower.

MATCH THE ITEMS TO THE MARKET

What do you find in a produce store or a fish market? Put each sticker in the store where it would be sold.

CREATE A THEME PARK

Lots of kids are having fun on the rides. Place the stickers on the matching shadows to complete the busy theme park!

HUNGRY HAMSTERS

The hamsters are hungry! Place stickers on each plate until each hamster has 3 seeds.

FILL IN THE FLOWERS

Add flower stickers to the trees to make all the trees look alike.

Use the stickers to fill in the maze. Put each sticker on the ▮ with the matching ★. Then, draw a line from ➡ to ➡ to solve the maze.

MATCH THAT TAIL!

Whose tail is that? Place each animal sticker in the box with its matching tail.

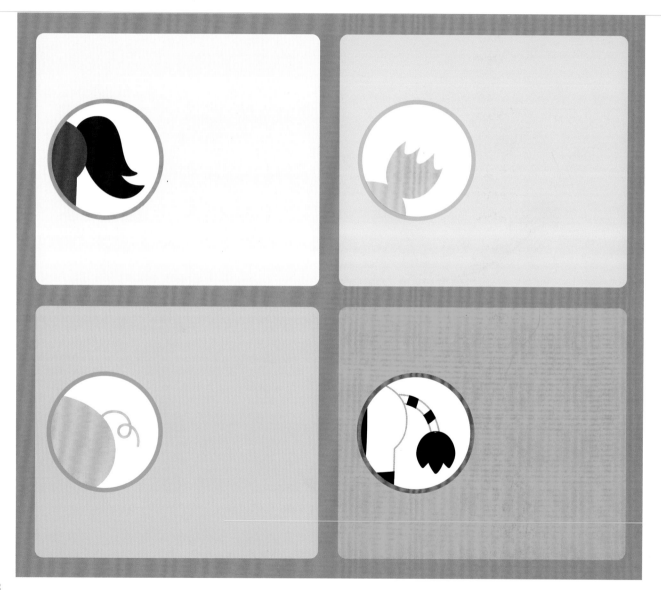